MY BEST FRIEND'S NEW FRIEND

FEELING LEFT OUT

You Choose the Ending

by Connie Colwell Miller • illustrated by Sofia Cardoso

Do you ever wish you could change a story or choose a different ending?

IN THESE BOOKS, YOU CAN!

Read along and when you see this:

WHAT HAPPENS NEXT?

Skip to the page for that choice, and see what happens.

In this story, Tife (TEE-fay) and Phoebe (FEE-bee) are best friends. Lately, Phoebe has been hanging out with Caitlin, and Tife feels left out. Will they work it out? YOU make the choices!

Tife and Phoebe are playing four square. Caitlin interrupts—for the third day in a row.

"Hey Phoebe, want to ride my scooter?" Caitlin asks.

"Sure!" Phoebe agrees.

WHAT HAPPENS NEXT?

→ If Tife watches the girls in silence, turn the page.

If Tife asks to join the girls, turn to page 20. ←

Phoebe runs off to join Caitlin. Tife begins to worry. What if Phoebe has more fun with Caitlin? What if Tife loses her best friend?

Tife isn't sure what to do. Then, she notices Damon sitting by the four square court all alone.

WHAT HAPPENS NEXT?

If Tife asks Damon to play, turn the page.
If Tife continues to worry, turn to page 16.

Tife stops worrying about Phoebe and Caitlin. Maybe she can make a new friend of her own.

"Hey, Damon," Tife says. "Want to play four square?"

Damon's face lights up. "Sure!" he says.

TURN TO PAGE 18 →

Tife yells at her friend in anger. "Oh, NOW you want to play with me? After you're bored with your new friend and her cool toy?"

Phoebe looks shocked and sad. "Tife—" she starts.

But Tife interrupts. "I don't want to play with you, Phoebe," she says.

TURN THE PAGE →

Phoebe walks away sadly. Being rude to Phoebe didn't make Tife any happier. In fact, it made her feel worse, and now she's alone.

Tife realizes she let her worry make her choices for her. As she heads off to apologize to Phoebe, she wishes she had made different choices.

THE END

→ Go to page 23. ←

Tife still feels upset and worried. But she really loves her best friend.

"Okay. I guess I'll play," Tife agrees.

The girls play in silence for a while.

TURN THE PAGE →

Finally, Tife talks to Phoebe. "Phoebe, it hurt my feelings when you left our game to play with Caitlin," she says.

"I'm sorry," Phoebe replies. "I had fun with Caitlin, but you'll always be my best friend."

Tife feels better now. She's glad she talked to Phoebe.

THE END

→ Go to page 23. ←

Tife watches Phoebe and Caitlin. They look like they are having a lot of fun together. Tife feels left out. She gets more and more upset with Phoebe.

Tife bounces the ball by herself for a while. She avoids Damon. After a while, Phoebe comes back.

"Want to play now?" Phoebe asks her.

WHAT HAPPENS NEXT?

If Tife gets mad at Phoebe, turn to page 8.
If Tife agrees to play, turn to page 12.

Tife has a great time playing with Damon. She even forgets her worry about Phoebe and Caitlin.

Later, Phoebe comes back and asks to join the game. Tife can tell that nothing has changed. Phoebe will always be her best friend—even if they don't always play together.

THE END

→ Go to page 23. ←

Tife is upset that Caitlin didn't ask her to play, too. Does that mean Caitlin doesn't like her? Or, worse, what if Phoebe likes Caitlin better than her? Will Tife lose her best friend?

Tife is worried, but she decides to ask a question. "Hey, Caitlin!" Tife says. "Can I play, too?"

TURN THE PAGE →

Caitlin smiles. "Sure! Do you want try my scooter?"
Tife sighs with relief. "I'd like that," she says.
Tife is proud of herself. She didn't let her worry make choices for her. Now, all three girls can play together.

THE END